THE Congratulations PROJECT

Copyright (c) 2018 by PALS Programs. All rights reserved.

No part of this publication may be reproduced, distributed, or transmitted in any form or by any means, including photocopying, recording, or other electronic or mechanical methods, without the prior written permission of PALS Programs, except in the case of brief quotations embodied in reviews and certain other non-commercial uses permitted by copyright law.

First Edition, 2018, PALS Programs, 4965 Grundy Way, Doylestown, PA 18902 Visit palsprograms.org

ISBN: 978-1-54392-577-7

Foreword

I didn't discover Camp PALS. Our son Gabe did. He was a sophomore at a school that required each student to perform a certain number of hours of community service. Gabe had spent several summers at a tennis camp run by a wonderful man named Julian Krinsky. It was Julian who suggested Gabe become a counselor at Camp PALS, where he would be paired for a week with a young adult with Down syndrome. He thought it would be a good experience for our boy. Gabe didn't know what to expect. For him, it was just a way to accumulate his "hours." So off he went. He was assigned a camper named Chris, a young man in his early twenties.

One week later, Richard and I drove to Camp PALS to pick up Gabe. Like him, we didn't know what to expect. There was a closing ceremony for the campers. When it was over, the campers' parents, many with tears in their eyes, thanked the counselors for giving their kids an experience that every child deserves but had never been available to theirs. I remember tearing up myself, so proud of our son and the profound impact he'd had on Chris and his family.

Gabe packed up his belongings, hugged all the campers and fellow counselors and we began the journey home. I told Gabe about my tears of pride. He described how moving it had been to see the transformation in each camper, having finally found a community where they were treated as equals and embraced. And then there was silence. It soon became clear that the boy in the backseat was not the same kid we had dropped off one week earlier. His words came slowly, as if he were processing this internal change. He said his time at Camp PALS ended up being the most formative experience of his life.

Before Camp PALS, he said he might have considered people with Down syndrome as disabled. He walked away from his experience feeling the campers were definitely different than most people, but in a way that taught him to see his world in a whole new light. As Gabe put it, "I left feeling they were some of the most compassionate people I will ever meet in my lifetime."

As you read the Congratulations letters in this book, you will see what Gabe saw that week. Each one is really a love letter to life and all its possibilities. And they are written not just to the new parents of babies with Down Syndrome, but to the babies themselves. As Jon puts it at the end of his, "I love my life. Your baby will too." As I read these letters, I find myself tearing up again. But this time, they are tears of gratitude from one parent to another. Gabe was 15 years old when he first became a counselor at Camp PALS. He spent several summers there, sharing memories with lots of campers. He was a good boy back then. Now he is a wonderful young man with a heightened sense of empathy and understanding for all people. I know that is because he had the great fortune to get to know a child like yours. So thank you from the bottom of my heart, and congratulations!

Meredith Vieira

Introduction

From the earliest moments, it's hard to imagine what anyone's life will be like. The triumphs, the struggles, the first love, the heartbreak. New babies bring a sense of pure wonder and excitement into the world, a miracle that holds so many possibilities for the future.

Hours after my brother, Jason, was born, my parents knew something was wrong. The doctor came in and announced Jason had Down syndrome. This news was followed by statistics, warnings, health concerns, and limitations that the doctors and the world placed upon him. The possibilities were stripped away, replaced with a sense of loss and fear.

This is one of many stories - families met with apologies, coping strategies, and generalizations. I've often wondered how my parents would have felt if they knew the impact Jason would have on me, on our family, on our community. Yes, it's hard to imagine what anyone's life will be like. But a glimpse at the future and its possibilities can bring back hope and allow us to dream again. And that can make all the difference.

The PALS vision is built on the concept that powerful friendships between those with and without Down syndrome can change perspectives that will eventually change the world. At PALS, we hear stories of transformation every day. Campers with Down syndrome grow in independence and develop new skills. Volunteers are challenged to change their expectations or even their life plan after spending a week paired with their Camper.

I created The Congratulations Project out of a need to combine these two experiences, both as a sibling who had been sculpted by my brother, and as a community member who witnessed the impact of individuals with Down syndrome every day. The Congratulations Project was an opportunity to share about the great value that people with Down syndrome bring to this world. But this wasn't a task that needed my voice. It needed theirs.

At each PALS program, our Campers are invited to write letters to new parents of babies with Down syndrome. We ask our Campers to share about their lives, their accomplishments, and their future. The only requirement is that our letters focus on the one word that is too often missing: Congratulations.

We collect hundreds of handwritten letters and ship them out to individual families as we receive requests. Our goal is that these letters, filled with the honest, personal words of PALS campers, will bring light and joy to new families, and all individuals across the world. This compilation highlights just a few of the letters we've collected. We hope you find this book in a doctor's office, in a hospital waiting room, on a friend's coffee table, and when you need it the most.

We hope you are changed by the words of our self-advocates, that you see the great value within every one, and that the next time you hear about a Down syndrome diagnosis, you think back to these words, smile, and say "Congratulations".

Jeni Newbury Ross

When a baby is diagnosed with Down syndrome, parents are confronted with coping strategies, given statistics, and often told

I'm sorry.

This book contains handwritten, original letters from individuals with Down syndrome to expecting or new parents whose baby has received the same diagnosis. They all begin with the same, simple message:

Congratulations.

Dear parent, :)

Congratulations on your new baby! My name is Jon, and I like to swim, and play kickball. In the future, I would like to work with the elderly and healthcare. I love my life. Your baby will too.

Sincerely,
Jon

Dear Parent,

Congratulations on your new Baby! My name is Maggie and I am proud of having a JOB, graduating a 2 year college program at ESU, and being on the swim team and doing gymnastics. I love my life because I have the best friends and family. I met Morgan in kindergarten. She didn't know until fifth grade — we are best of friends we go to Camp PALS together. I know that your baby will have good friends like Morgan. I want your baby to know that they are intelligent, nice, outgoing and will be supported be modest be happy be excited

Sincerely
Maggie

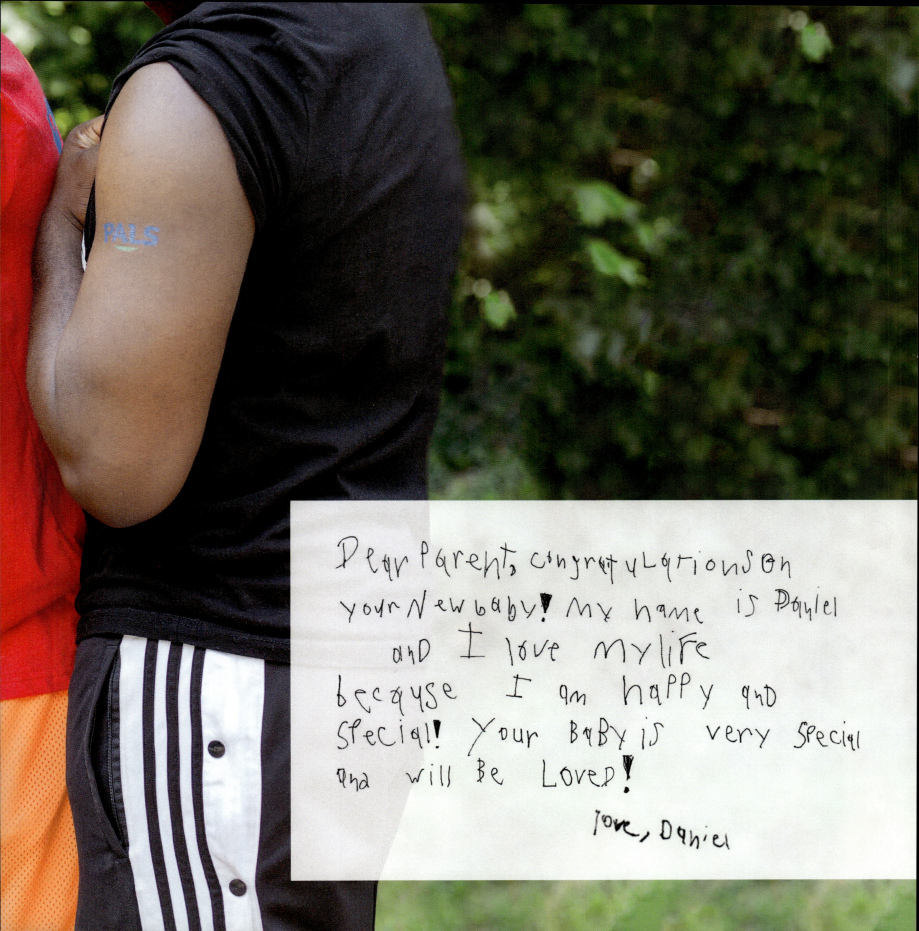

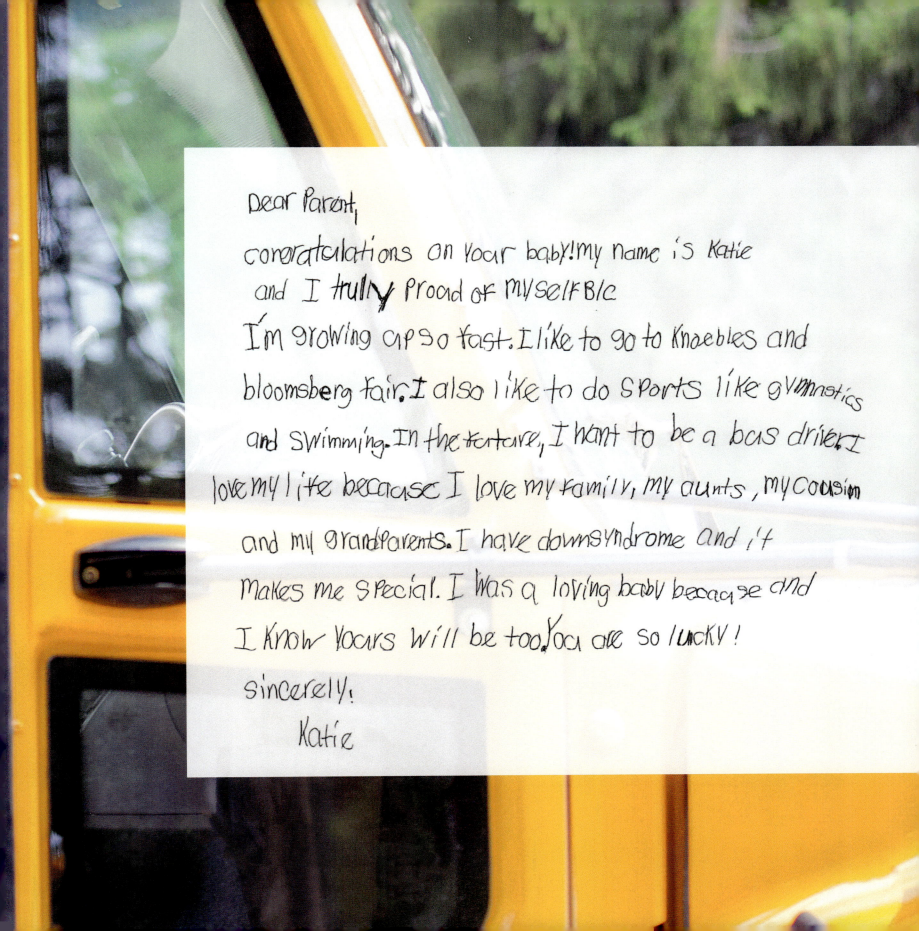

Dear Parent,

congratulations on your baby! My name is Katie and I trully proud of myself B/c I'm growing up so fast. I like to go to Knoebles and bloomsberg fair. I also like to do sports like gymnastics and swimming. In the fertare, I want to be a bus driver. I love my life because I love my family, my aunts, my cousin and my grandparents. I have downsyndrome and it makes me special. I was a loving baby because and I know yours will be too. You are so lucky!

sincerely,
Katie

Dear Parent.
Congratulations on your new baby! My name is Olivia. God Love me because I Am me. I Love my Life. I want to be a wedding planner and a Preacher. I like to work with specla needs kids and people
　　　　　　Sincerely, Olivia

Dear parent congratulation on your new baby. My name is meg and I am proud of my family because they love me. I like to play basketball and dance. In the future i want to have a job at a restaurant. I love my life because my family takes good care of me. I love them for it. congratulations on having a baby who will grow up and be awesome.

sincerely, meg

Dear Parent, Congratualations on your new baby! My name is Nicholas. I Love my Life because I Swimming at the Ridley high school. I really good Swimmers because I really good doing butterfly. My Favorite Muisc is Justin bieber I am really Loved by My Parent I am cute AT Camp PALS I Made a Friend named Tyler. He is the Best Because He Makes me Feel Loved and Special. I Love Camp PALS Because everyone Loves Me. Yes I have downsydrome but I wouldn't change a thing about Me. I Loves Who I am.

Love
Nick

Dear Parent,

Congratulations on your new baby. My name is Rebecca and I am proud of graduating of class of 2015. I like to Dance and gymnacias. In the future I want to be a Pro Dancer. I Love my life because I have great friends and Great counselors. When I was born I was the same size as a peanut. And now I Dance for 15 years.

Sincerely,
Rebecca

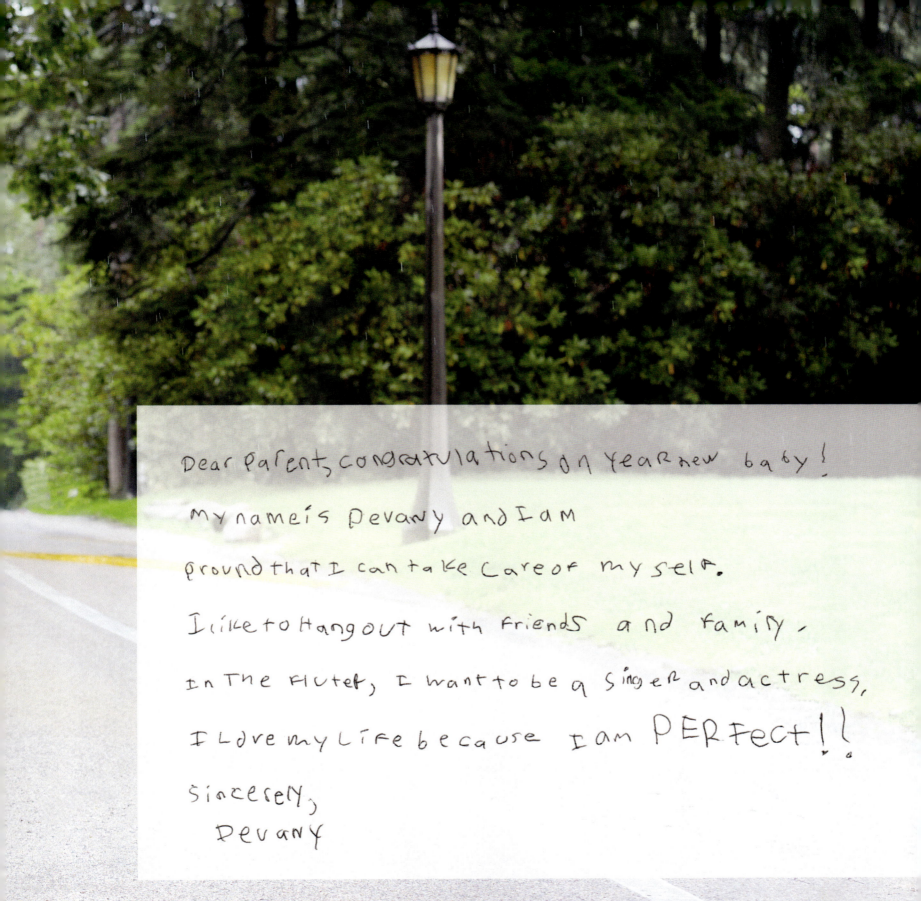

Dear Parents, congratulations on year new baby! My name is Devany and I am pround that I can take care of myself. I like to hang out with friends and family. In the future, I want to be a singer and actress. I love my life because I am PERFECT!!

Sincerely,
Devany

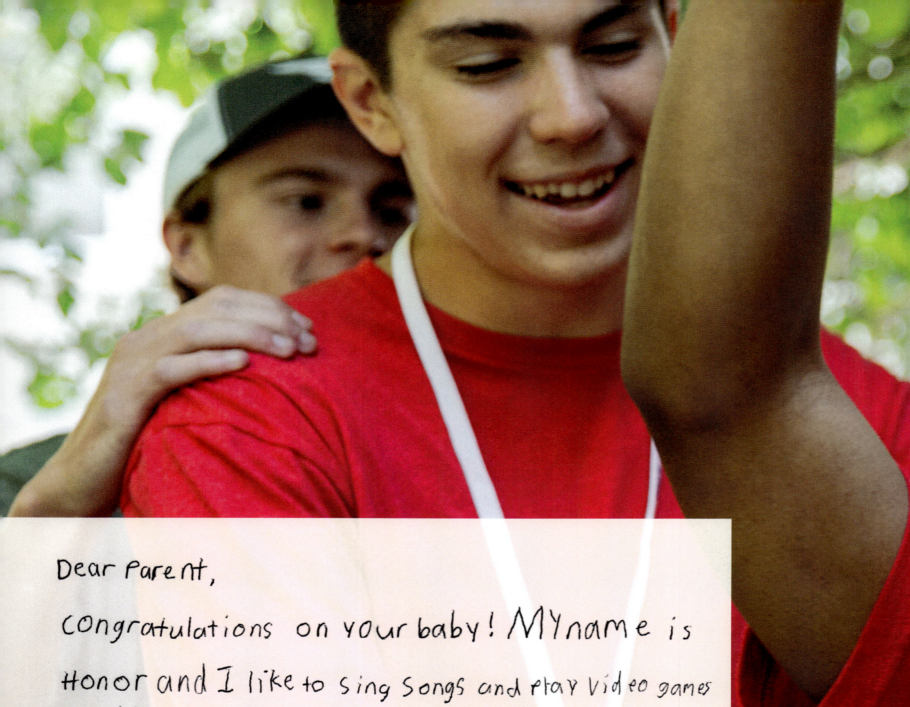

Dear Parent,

Congratulations on your baby! My name is Honor and I like to sing songs and play video games. In the future I want to clean my room. I love my life because of xbox games

Honor

Dear parent
Congratulation on you new baby
I am Gradared from High school
helping kids and trying to be a
better cook. Save my recipes on
pintereso Even though I have
a down syndrome I can still do
speal things. I am so Proud of you
in the futere I want to I wonk at the day care
I Love my life becase I have a family who
Love me I have a twins sister Her name
is Cassie I relly Love my twins sister
so so so macn

   Love Callie

Dear Parent

Congratulations on your new baby! My Name is Scotty And I am 15 years old with down syndrome. My Life is Really awsome because I geat Mad cool nicknames, I am Really good at all sports and play crazy instruments. I am Really Honest, caring and I Love my Family. I am also awsome at makeing new Friends. I wish the best of Luck with your new bady, YOUR Life Just got pretty darn cool.

Love Scotty "scooter"

Dear Parent
Congratulations on your new baby! my name is Sarah and i love my mom and sister. i love to care for people. I love my life because i was adopted. i want to today care of my family. i care for my dogs i am proud of my family. you are great.
love Sarah

Dear Parent,

Congratulations on your new baby! My name is AnnaRose and I am proud of my involvement in Sports. I like to play basketball, soccer, cheerleading, and swimming. In fact I am coaching kids' soccer in the summer. In the future, I want to help kids play sports and to become pros. I love my life because I love my family. My sister Rachael has Down Syndrome too. She is perfect just like me.

Sincerely,
AnnaRose

Dear Parent,
Congratulations! My name is Patrick and I am proud of making freinds and graduation from High School. In the future, I want to go to UC Davis and to be a director. There's no reason to be scared of having a kid with Down syndrome as long as you love them, they will love you back. Good luck and have fun!!
Love,
Patrick

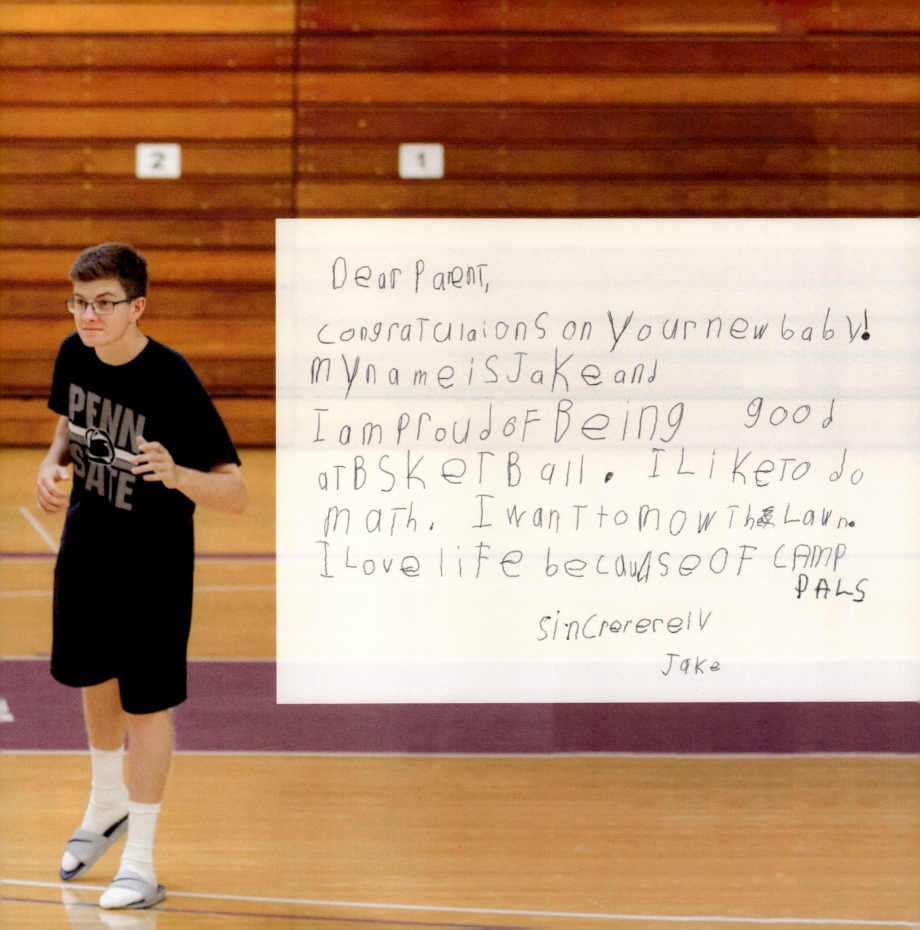

Dear Parent,

Congratulaions on your new baby! My name is Jake and I am proud of Being good at BSKetBall. I Like to do math. I want to mow the Lawn. I Love life because of CAMP PALS

Sincrererely
Jake

Dear Parent,

Congratulations on your new baby! My name is Mackenzie and I am proud of being myself and trying to find out who I am. In the future, I want to be famous for something that I love. I like to ride Horses, play video games, watching tv, and etc. I Also want to be a leader for the younger generations in my country that is because I love my life. My friends and all of them call me M-dawg

love,

Mackenzie

Dear Parent,
Congratulations on your new baby! My name is Jocelyn and I like to sing and Dance. In the future, I want to move out and get a job. I love my life because I love family and everybody is so nice to me.
            Sincerely Jocelyn

Dear Parent,

Congratulations on your new baby! My name is Cody and I love my life because I get supported for my dance, school, softball, song writing, cooking. I like to be twinning with my camp bro, I was on "So you think you can dance, I met famous people, I'm already in college for dance, cause I have a dance backround. I'm 21, so I can drink "now" I only have 1 peer week. I know how scary is to having a baby but don't forget, you have support from all of us. I love my life. Don't give up what you started.

Sincerely,

Cody :)

Queridos papas,

Muchas felicidades de tener su nuevo bebé. Mi nombre es Mónica y yo estoy orgullosa de ser estudiante y hacer amable con los demas, Me gusta hacer amigo y hablar con ellos, en mi futura quiero casarme con mi novio y de tener un coche para quiero mi vida porqué soy buena conmigo yo misma, por tener una familia unida qué hizo dios y tener amor con mi familia

Sinceramente, Mónica

Dear parent,
congratiuaions on your new baby
My name is Taylor and
I am Proud of My good grades an
being a good aunt.
I like to hang out with My boyfriend
and friends

1. I am good at
dancing and singing.

2. In the future i would like
to get Married and have
one child. i also Would
like to become a. teacher

3. good luck with your
baby. dont be scared
be happy because they
are going to be great and
successful. You I Love
                Taylor

Dear Parents, congratulations on your new baby! my name is Zachary and I am proud of your new baby, in the future I want to be a model. I like to congratuation on new baby. I love my life because how I complish on what I do in high school like getting my deploma. and also being a great guy in the future! having a baby is hard to handle like burp, poop, change the baby. but most of times is when they still a baby you love them when they be a teen you fight alot but finaly when they turn twenty year old gratuade high school and to college they leave. but they never have a better mom and dad have fun with the new baby.

Sincerly

Zachary

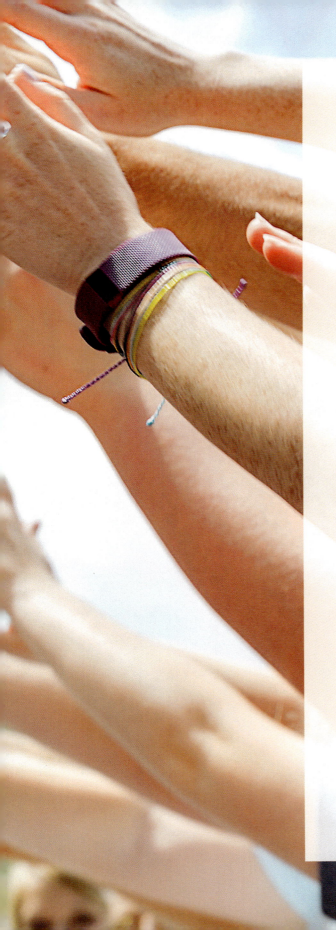

Dear Parent,

Congratulations on your new baby! My name is Lauren and I am proud of that I have Downs drayme because it makes me feel good. I like to play games and hanging with my friends. In the future, I want to teach Special needs kids to learn how to dance while they have special needs. I love my life because I have a lot of friends and being the best at everything. I also attended college at East Stroudsburg University for 3 years and it helped me to learn about living skills and to be an adult. I am also proud of being a hostess at a restaurant. I also worked at East Hills Middle School and I work in the kitchen. My advice is to love your child as much as my mom loves me.

Sincerely,
Lauren

Dear parent,

congrates on your newborn baby and my name is Jason 27 yrs old enjoy guitar, singing, and knowing it was hard to be in your Position of being a mother. I have a baby neicee and still learing how to be a uncle too. I wrote a speech about my grandparents because they are my Insairation to me too! I'm proud of success at babysiting and reading books to kids. In the future, I want to be an national airlines Pilot. I love my life because I have Down syndrome to, and I cant wait to tell you what down syndrome means to your new baby.

P.S. be yourslef

Jason

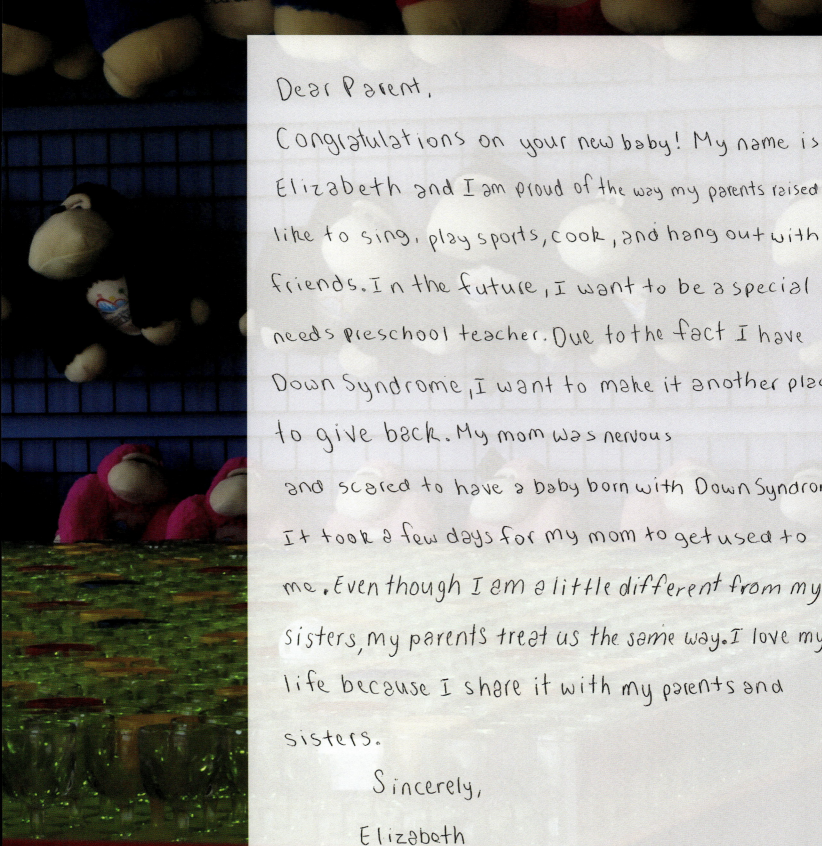

Dear Parent,

Congratulations on your new baby! My name is Elizabeth and I am proud of the way my parents raised me. I like to sing, play sports, cook, and hang out with friends. In the future, I want to be a special needs preschool teacher. Due to the fact I have Down Syndrome, I want to make it another place to give back. My mom was nervous and scared to have a baby born with Down Syndrome. It took a few days for my mom to get used to me. Even though I am a little different from my sisters, my parents treat us the same way. I love my life because I share it with my parents and sisters.

   Sincerely,

   Elizabeth

Dear Parents,

I am happy for you to have a baby that has Down Syndrome, I am Jeremy and I have Down Syndrome and I am 23. I hope that your baby is going to be born in April, because my birthday is April to. My experience with my birth is different from your baby's birth because no one at first knew what Down Syndrome meant. They were scared of me when they found out that I had Down Syndrome, I don't want you to be scared and I do want you to educate yourself on the Down Syndrome part. I hope that you're baby will be in Camp Pals when he or she grows up. Also my experience being born my mom and dad They leaned on to God with everything to make my birth possible. I want you to lean on to God to help with everything to make your birth possible, When your baby grows up it does not matter if your baby is going to be gay, straight, black and white.

I would like to know if your baby when he or she grows up to be into marvel movies or harry potter movies, because that's my favorite movies.

Congrats
Jeremy

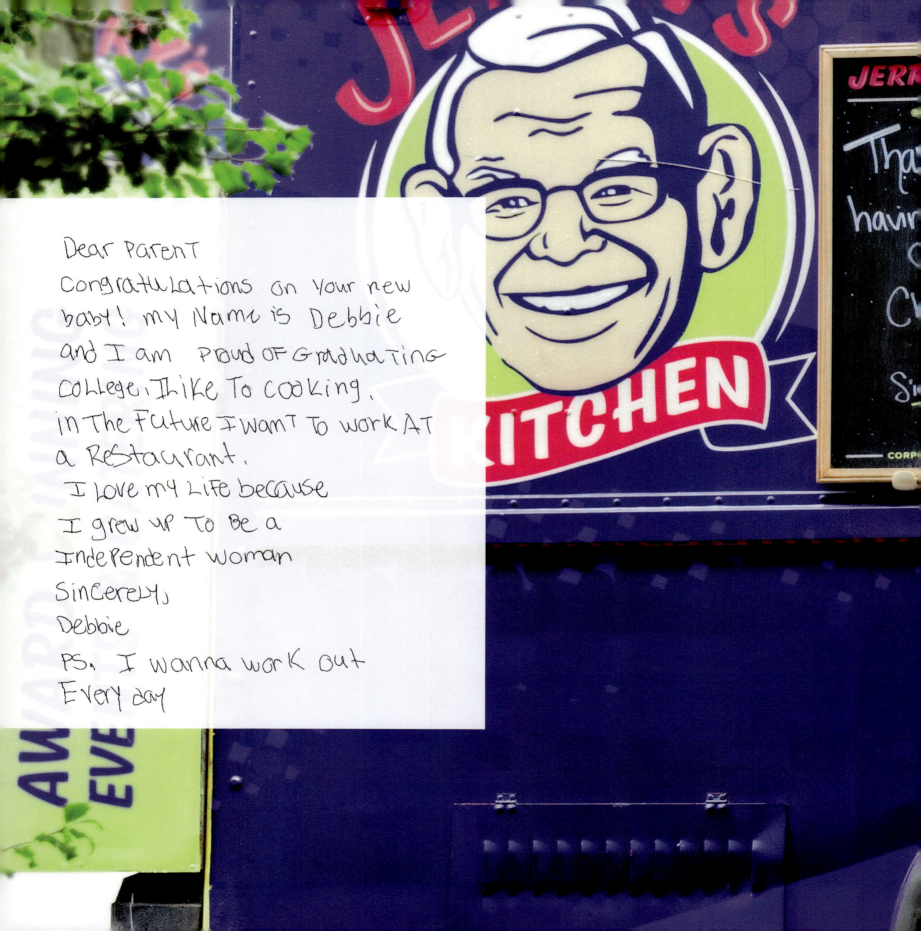

Dear Parent,

Congratulations on your new baby! My name is Zoë and I have a rare case of down-syndrome that is called Mosiac down-syndrome. I am very special because I learned how to be independent quickly than others that have down-syndrome, and I am very good in the educational world. I learned how to read much earlier, and I learned how to write much earlier as well. I am proud of myself because I accomplished a lot through many years. In the future I hope to become a special education teacher and a psycologist. I love my life because I have a family that supports me and my friends love me for me and they never want me to change who I am.

        Sincerely,

        Zoe

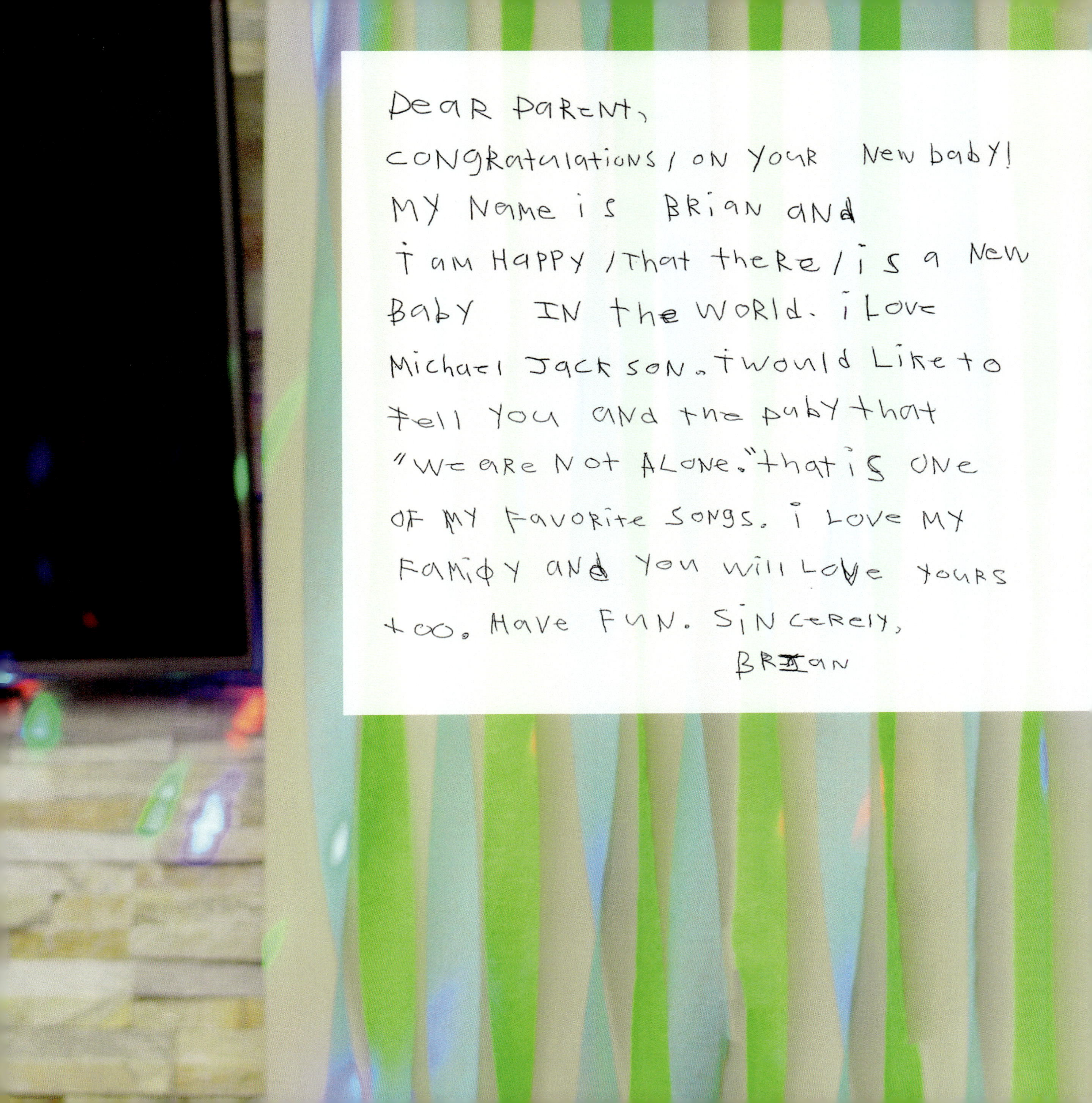

Dear Parent,

Congratulations! on your new baby! My name is Brian and I am happy /that there /is a new baby in the world. I love Michael Jackson. I would like to tell you and the baby that "We are not alone." That is one of my favorite songs. I love my family and you will love yours too. Have fun. Sincerely,

Brian

Dear Parent,

Congratulations on you're baby! My name is Candace and I am proud of my life because I have two parents who rise me to be a indpendent young lady. I like to play field hockey for 7 years and I am a professional player. In the neer future, I want to be a Pastery Chef because I love to be in the kitchen all the time with my mom. I love my life because I like to read book's a lot and love and support from my parents. I went to college for two years I learned how to live on my own without my parents.

Sincerely
Candace

Dear Parent,
Congratulations on your new baby!!
My name is Sarah. Don't be flabbergasted about the new baby it will be okay bc (because) I am here for you and I am so excited for you! I like to eat, dance, sing, act, and cooking! In my future I want to be an actress. Because I love to hear all of their voices! I love my life bc (because) it is so special and unique. I know you are really excited about the baby! And I am so proud of you! I hope the baby loves hot dogs they are so good! This year I went to prom! It is so beautiful! I hope the baby will be magical in our hearts because the baby will be special in your lifes! I hope the baby will be special like you!

Your friend,
Sarah

Dear Parent, Congratulations on your new baby! My name is MAC and I am proud to be a senior in high school. Im going to college at Bowling Green. I love my job at Sloopy's sports cafe. I like making my own money. When I grow up I want to live in san fransisco. My Birth Parent are Chinase, but live with my new mom and sister kit. I Love them very much and they Love me. GO CAVS!!!
LOVE:
MAC

Dear Parent,

Congratualtions on your new baby. My name is Mary and I am proud of being Down syndrome b/c we are special. We are free to do wantever we want to enjoy life. I love my life because we learn new things like school. I am happy for you because you will have a new baby. I know how you feel sad and scerd you don't know if your child will make it but I have faith in you. Your child may have open heart sugrey and leukemia b/c I have it in me. My mom and dad use to be sad and scerd because they think I won't make it but I know I am brave I am a survivor in my life. It will be hard b/c people will think you are different a person and a azauing person as who you are don't let people put you down you are special to your friends and family. You will have a happy life it's your life make it happan start your life now. people will be inspired for your kid or yours. be yourself you are breteful to others. you did it you have a kid enjoy it help others be kind, honset, selfes, and being brave

Sincerely Mary

Authors

Debbie Ade	Zachary Day	Scotty Lesmes
Katie Allen	Jeremy Diskint	Nick Luther
Mónica Arce	Devany Fabula	Jocelyn Maldonado
Mackenzie Bockwoldt	Patrick Foraker	Jon Mattern
Mary Borman	Taylor Garfield	Jason Newbury
Daniel Borowy	Honor Griffin	Zoe Phillpotts
Cody Carlson	Meg Kensil	Sarah Platt
Brian Ciccantelli	Elizabeth Kerrigan	AnnaRose Rubright
Lauren Coni	Jake Klouser	Mac Stephenson
Candace Cosgrove	Rebecca Knight	Sarah Sudmeier
Maggie Cunliffe	Olivia Landis	Callie Weimer

Acknowledgments

Photography:

With sincere gratitude and appreciation to Michelle Kilgore for her photography and support.
Special thanks for photograph submissions from:
AJ Abelman, Colton Davies, Elizabeth Miller, Sofie Palumbo, Tien Vo, and the Norton Family

Design & Layout:

Colton Davies

PALS Programs began in 2004. The vision was clear—changing perspectives through relationships built on shared experiences. We paired up young adults with Down syndrome one-on-one with their peers to have fun, grow as individuals, and to build transformative friendships along the way.

Our programming begins with Camp PALS, our week-long summer sleep away camps held on college campuses across the country. The experiences continue with PALS Adventures, weekend getaways during our off-season at retreat centers, resorts, and rented homes. And we strengthen our community with The Congratulations Project, reaching out to congratulate and welcome new families of babies with Down syndrome through letters written by our Campers.

PALS has shaped the lives of hundreds of individuals over the past years. Half of us have Down syndrome, but all of us know the value of friendship, the thrill of being on a team, and the best place to experience summer. Together, we challenge each other to be a little better, and to see the world a little differently, with each passing year.

We seek to build a community of passionate people —of those who step out of their comfort zones, those who take time to reach out to others, and those who celebrate the joy in every moment. Our work is dedicated to the Down syndrome community, but our impact is not. We believe that this place, this family, can challenge others to see their world a little differently.

We promise to keep growing—to find new areas that need our passion and genuine energy, to age with those individuals who have grown up with us, and to give even the youngest members of our community a sense of hope and a feeling of welcome.

Together, we will build a world where **friends** count more than **chromosomes**.